Original title:
Beneath the Winter Stars

Copyright © 2024 Creative Arts Management OÜ
All rights reserved.

Author: Sophia Kingsley
ISBN HARDBACK: 978-9916-94-614-5
ISBN PAPERBACK: 978-9916-94-615-2

Nights of Cosmic Stillness

The snowflakes twirled, dressed in their best,
While penguins played poker, feeling quite blessed.
An owl wearing glasses, perched high on a tree,
Shouted, "Who? Who? Time for a spree!"

The squirrels donned hats, all furry and warm,
Debating the merits of snowball alarm.
Cosmic giggles echo in the chilly air,
As comet tails race without a single care.

The Heartbeat of the Snowy Cosmos

A snowman with swagger, he waved with a grin,
Challenging snowflakes for a dance-off to begin.
The stars all chuckled at his frosty flair,
While snowballs flew by without a hint of despair.

A moose played the banjo, a cat sang along,
They harmonized sweetly, as bright as a song.
The universe winked at this wacky delight,
As laughter exploded through the crisp, frosty night.

Dance of the Frozen Celestials

The snowmen shimmied with sticks arms spread wide,
As the moonlight chuckled, a bright, cheeky guide.
Frosty feet shuffled, tapping out a beat,
While stars joined the fun, never missing a beat.

In this icy ballet, the penguins rocked out,
With snowflakes all spinning, swirling about.
The cosmos watched closely, with popcorn in hand,
Amused by the antics of this frosty band.

Winter's Elysium of Stars

The fir trees were dressed in diamonds and fluff,
As the rabbits made snowballs, their aim, quite tough.
One threw with a flourish, it flew through the air,
And splatted the snowman, who just couldn't care.

The stars sang a chorus, twinkling with glee,
While ice fish did wiggle in a cosmic spree.
In this winter wonder, all creatures so bright,
Turned the coldest of evenings to pure comic delight.

The Dreamer's Nocturne of Ice

In dreams so cold, I skate with glee,
A penguin lead, he'd drink my tea.
The moon shakes hands with frosty pines,
And jokes about their icy lines.

The stars, like sprinkles, fall in piles,
I slip on ice and greet their smiles.
My sled is pulled by fluffy cats,
Who wear their scarves, like silly hats.

Frigid Lullabies and Cosmic Rides

The universe hums a chilly tune,
While comets dance with spoons and prune.
I ride my thoughts on frozen beams,
Chasing the frosty ice-cream dreams.

The snowflakes giggle, twirl, and spin,
Catching my nose, it tickles within.
I tell the trees to take a seat,
They wave their branches, feel the beat.

Winter's Breath and Cosmic Glints

A radiant frost creeps on the ground,
While squirrels wear jackets, twirling round.
The icy breath of winter's fate,
Tells snowmen jokes; they laugh, they wait.

As stars erupt in laughter bright,
The cosmos winks, a merry sight.
My toes complain, they rant in blue,
I dance with penguins; they join too.

Evening's Polished Ice

The evening glimmers, ice so fine,
I slip and slide, it's quite divine.
With frozen puddles full of cheer,
I strut my stuff, and grab a beer.

The stars above roll their big eyes,
As I make castles; the ice complies.
I wear a coat of snowy fluff,
This frosty dance is just enough.

Secrets of the Frostbitten Horizon

A penguin in a tux, quite dapper and neat,
He waddles and slips, on his frozen feet.
He dreams of a dance on the glimmering ice,
With snowflakes as partners, oh isn't that nice?

The snowmen gossip, their hats all askew,
They trade frozen secrets, we'd laugh if we knew.
They say winter's chill brings a humorous freeze,
A joke's just a snowball, so toss it with ease!

Glittering Mirage of Arctic Dreams

A seal on a float, with a splash and a grin,
He claims he's the king of this frosty din.
With ice as his throne and the sun's little beams,
He pops up with jokes, or so it seems!

The northern lights dance, and they flicker with glee,
They tease the poor ravens, 'Just wait, you will see!'
The owls roll their eyes, while the foxes just trot,
In this sparkling world, there's laughter—quite a lot!

Songs of Darkness and Icy Wonders

In shadows where snowflakes do take their sweet flight,
The rabbits tell stories, oh what a delight!
With ears that perk up at the silliest tunes,
They frolic and hop, beneath glowing moons.

The icebergs are grinning, they've seen all the fun,
As seals crack up jokes, while they bask in the sun.
Their laughter resounds through the crisp, chilly air,
A tale as old as time, but with flair beyond compare!

The Brightness of Cold Horizons

At dawn, the icicles shimmer, a naughty delight,
The squirrels plot mischief, oh what a sight!
With snowball catapults, they take aim at their pals,
While laughter erupts from the nearby snow-caps.

The snow is their canvas, each paw prints a jest,
As winter's own jesters, they play and they rest.
With giggles and chaos, they revel and cheer,
In this frosty kingdom, there's nothing to fear!

A Dream Wrapped in Ice

In frosty air, penguins prance,
While snowmen waltz in a goofy dance.
They slip on ice, oh what a sight,
Chasing snowflakes in pure delight.

A snowball fight goes terribly wrong,
Snowflakes fall like a silly song.
Every toss and every throw,
Covers folks in a frosty glow.

Hot cocoa spills, a marshmallow square,
Puppies leap, with snow in their hair.
Each frosty breath a puff of fun,
Winter antics for everyone.

Laughter echoes through the chill,
As everyone tumbles down a hill.
The ice may crack, the laughter's loud,
A jolly bunch, snow-covered crowd.

Night's Unfurling of Frozen Mysteries

In the frozen night, owls wear hats,
Noses poking through the snow like rats.
They hoot and howl at the twinkling light,
While snowflakes fall, so fluffy, so white.

A squirrel in boots, attempting to skate,
Slides and slips with a cheeky fate.
The moon giggles, a cheeky cop,
As he catches the critters in a frosty flop.

Icicles twinkling, like teeth on a grin,
Frogs in tuxedos, about to begin.
They croak a tune, a chilly serenade,
As snowflakes gather, a soft parade.

Frosty keeps secrets, but whispers in glee,
Tickling noses, as funny as can be.
The stars blink down, wearing big smiles,
While laughter echoes through snowy miles.

When Stars Kiss the Frozen Earth

The snowflakes dance with wild delight,
As stars giggle in the frosty night.
One tripped over a cold, white mound,
And whispered secrets, all around.

A snowman grins with a silly hat,
While rabbits hop, 'Hey, how about that!'
A comet sneezes, causing a flare,
And space squirrels scurry without a care.

The moonlight winks through icy trees,
Tickling the branches with a chilly breeze.
The ground is slippery, oh what a show,
As stars keep chuckling at the snow below.

A Universe Enfolded in Stillness

In the quiet void, a star spots a snack,
A twinkling donut in the cosmic black.
It rolls and tumbles, what a surprise,
While aliens giggle with wide-open eyes.

The planets shuffle, they can't keep still,
Jokingly dodging the great cosmic chill.
One lost its ring in a friendly chase,
Said, 'I'll wear this comet, it's a stylish grace!'

Galaxies swirl in a jazzy dance,
While stardust sprinkles like glitter in a trance.
Asteroids chuckle, bouncing nearby,
Making grand wishes as they zoom by.

Celestial Paths and Crystal Light

When meteors streak, they draw silly lines,
Like cosmic doodles on galactic signs.
Stars hum tunes with a sparkling glow,
While Space Cats prance in the cosmic show.

The Milky Way giggles, a creamy delight,
As comets parade in the shimmering night.
One lost its tail in a game of tease,
Said, 'Next time I'll try to aim with ease!'

With laughter as bright as the twinkling sphere,
Each cosmic critter holds joy and cheer.
In the vastness, the fun doesn't cease,
For the universe's silly never finds peace.

The Sigh of a Snow-Draped Night

A whisper floats through the frosty air,
A snowy owl, quite hard to spare.
It hoots a joke to the chilly breeze,
While penguins shuffle, trying to please.

The trees, they shiver, tickled by night,
With icicles hanging, what a sight!
They chime like bells with a plinky plonk,
As frosty giggles around them donk.

The stars peek down, with a wink and grin,
Saying, 'Join the fun, let the frolic begin!'
So under the snow, all creatures unite,
In the winter's laughter, pure delight.

Star-Studded Frost

The night is cold, my nose turns red,
I dance around, but trip on sled.
The stars above, they twinkle bright,
I swear they giggle at my plight.

A snowman waves with carrot nose,
He watches closely as my pants froze.
I chase snowflakes, try to catch,
But all I get is a frosty scratch.

Hot cocoa in hand, I take a sip,
But watch out! I take a tiny dip.
With marshmallows floating like tiny boats,
I daydream of skiing down icy moats.

As I sip, a snowball flies through air,
It hits my friend with a cheeky flair.
Laughter echoes through wintry night,
As we all play, stars gleam in light.

Echoes of the Cold Constellations

In the dark, I slip on ice,
But all I hear is chuckles, nice.
Moonbeams giggle, shine so bright,
As I tumble in this snowy plight.

My scarf gets tangled, what a mess,
I look like a winter fashion stress.
The stars above wink with delight,
At my antics that light up the night.

A snowball fight breaks out with glee,
I duck and roll, feel so carefree.
The constellations all unite,
To watch this joyful, silly sight.

With frozen toes, I shout hooray,
As I fall over, my friends will play.
Under frost, our laughter sings,
Echoes of joy, winter's gifts it brings.

A Blanket of Cosmic Stillness

The ground is soft with snowy fluff,
I attempt to make a snow angel, tough.
But instead I roll, get stuck like glue,
I'm now a snowball, oh what to do?

Stars above wink and twist with mirth,
While I ponder my ego's dearth.
The stillness wraps me, makes me snore,
What a silly time, who could want more?

In my winter coat, I shimmy and sway,
Trying to dance but lose my way.
Constellations laugh at my goofy moves,
As I groan in snow, my body improves.

A hot drink waits on the table nearby,
I've earned a treat, that's no lie.
With buttered popcorn for the show,
We toast to winter's fun and frosty glow.

The Glimmer of Ice and Light

Stars are glimmering like frosty tales,
As I slip on ice and unleash my wails.
The cold air surrounds me, crisp and bright,
Even the frost seems to laugh tonight.

In the moonlight, my friends start to sing,
With hilarious voices, it's a silly fling.
We build a fort, a castle of snow,
Till one brave soul starts a cotton-ball throw.

A comet flashes by with a start,
Just like my friend who fell with a dart.
With giggles echoing through the still,
Who knew winter could bring such a thrill?

So here we dance under ice's charm,
As snowflakes twirl, they keep us warm.
The glimmer of laughter lights the night,
As stars above shine with pure delight.

Whispers Hidden in Frozen Shadows

In the chill, penguins dance,
Sliding on ice with advance.
Snowflakes giggle, spiraling round,
They trip on their tails, fall to the ground.

Snowmen wait with carrot noses,
Telling jokes that nobody knows.
Starlit laughter fills the night,
As frosty friends join in delight.

Candles flicker, warming hearts,
While frosty creatures share their parts.
Elves on skis, with stylish flair,
They tumble and roll without a care.

The moon peeks through the chilly mist,
As snowflakes laugh, they can't resist.
Winter's fun in frozen glee,
With whispers soft, like singing bees.

Captured in Lunar Silence

Under silver skies, we peek,
The owl hoots, a bit unique.
Snowball fights and fluffed-up hats,
A bear wearing socks? Oh, imagine that!

Starlight jokes and frozen pies,
Turtle races under the skies.
Mixing cocoa with giggly cheer,
As frosty pals gather near.

Lunar beams bring whispered fun,
What will happen? Let's just run!
Snowflakes wink and flutter by,
With chortles echoing, oh my, oh my!

A snow angel, sprawled on ground,
Wonders if others are around.
"Did I make my wings too wide?"
The laughter spreads; they cannot hide.

A Pathway through Celestial Frost

Frosty footprints lead us near,
Laughter echoes, warm with cheer.
The moon is grinning, light and bright,
As squirrels chatter, ready for flight.

Snowflakes spin in playful dance,
While snowmen join with a goofy stance.
They tell silly stories wrapped in fluff,
Claiming winter's not quite tough enough!

A frozen pond reflects the stars,
With skating lessons, not forcars.
Penguins wobble, then take a spill,
Chasing laughter, they get their fill.

In this chill with winter's bite,
Jokes are shared, all feel so light.
With ice cream cones of snow to savor,
We jog and laugh, it's our favorite flavor.

Illuminated by Frigid Gleams

Icicles dangle, sparkling bright,
They glint and glimmer, what a sight!
Snowflakes twirl in chilly air,
Making snow angels without a care.

Giggles bounce off frosty walls,
As we skate, someone giggling falls.
Laughter rumbles, a swirling cheer,
Oh winter fun, we hold you dear!

A light-up snowman wins the race,
With blinking eyes and a funny face.
He sings a tune, off-key and proud,
As the winter's laughter gathers a crowd.

Twinkling stars above do tease,
With frosty whispers in the breeze.
Warm hearts collide in chilly play,
As we cherish this bright winter day.

Icy Echoes Under the Galaxy

Snowflakes dance like tiny ninjas,
They land on noses, soft and fringed.
Winter's breath, a frosty giggle,
As penguins slide and finally cringe.

Frosty breath turns into clouds,
Laughter bubbles, it's time to play.
Chasing snowmen in fluffy shrouds,
Who knew cold could be this gay?

Snowball fights in a swirling spree,
Hats get flung like a UFO.
Silly selfies by the tree,
All together in clustered row!

But watch out for the frozen ground,
One slip, and down like a ton of bricks!
Giggling heals the icy sound,
As we leap like kids with funny tricks!

A Canvas of Night's Crystals

Glittering stars in a darkened sky,
Call me a comet—whoosh on by!
Snowmen wearing a carrot nose,
Laughing as they freeze in pose.

Squirrels in parkas, all bundled tight,
Laugh and whisper secrets at night.
Icicles hanging, they pretend to sing,
And I join in, what a funny fling!

Pine trees twinkle with their bling,
A winter crown fit for a king.
Snowflakes wear coats of silvery sheen,
Dancing like stars, all pristine!

We tackle each other and roll in the snow,
What a sight with cheeks all aglow!
Chasing shadows, we're silly and bold,
Creating a story that never gets old!

Frozen Silence in Celestial Depths

The quiet crunch as we march in a line,
Snowflakes whisper, 'Come join the fun!'
Riding sleds down hills we define,
With laughter ringing, the night has begun!

Yet, look out for a branch, low and stooped,
A smack in the face—oh, how we drooped!
But laughter bursts as we tumble and fall,
Snowball rockets fly, who will take the brawl!

Stars twinkle above with a wink and a grin,
A cacophony of joy, it's where we begin.
Our hats blow off like they're seeking a flight,
While we roll in laughter, what a silly sight!

Frosted fingers give sticky high-fives,
As snowmen hold their carrots with pride.
In this frozen world, humor thrives,
A winter wonderland where silliness can't hide!

The Night Sky's Diamond Tapestry

Stars shimmer like sugar on toast,
A frosty feast of silly cheer.
Hot cocoa mugs we all toast,
Topped with marshmallows, oh dear!

Our boots stomp down on crunchy snow,
Making shadows that dance and play.
Snowflakes swirl—don't go too slow,
Or you'll miss the fun, hip-hip-hooray!

We build a snow fort, 'cause why not?
Defending it from an enemy team!
Snowball launches are what we sought,
With giggles echoing like a dream!

But suddenly, someone throws too hard,
A snowball hits the unsuspecting bard!
Laughter erupts, we're all a bit wild,
In this winter scene, every heart's a child!

Echoes of the Frozen Sky

A snowman with a funny hat,
Stood tall until the cat sat.
He wobbled, then went with a flop,
Who knew frost could make a prop?

The squirrels wear little boots,
While plotting how to steal our fruits.
They giggle high on frosty trees,
Eating acorns like it's cheese.

On icy slopes, we slide so fast,
That mitten lost, we laugh and gasped.
Yet with each tumble, surely, we'd
Gain giggles, not just bruises, indeed.

The moon peeks from behind a cloud,
We're all asleep; she thinks she's loud.
With shivers and snorts we doze,
While dreams of snowball fights then rose.

Under the Heavy Gaze of Night

A penguin in a winter coat,
Thought he could surely float.
But every time he jumps with style,
It's more of a belly flop and a smile.

In woolly socks, we dance around,
Tripping over dogs that abound.
The frost bites, but we laugh and play,
As cocoa spills out on the tray.

Twinkling lights are strung so bright,
Climbing ladders gives such a fright.
With every twist we try to find,
The best spot is always behind.

A snowball fight erupts in cheer,
An avalanche of laughter near.
As one rogue snowball hits my face,
I laugh it off; let the fun embrace!

Starlit Chill in Every Breath

The stars blink down like playful eyes,
As frost kisses our cheeks—what a surprise!
We moonwalk on the icy ground,
While giggling at the cold we've found.

A toasty fire is where we meet,
But roasting marshmallows? Quite the feat!
The flames jump high like a merry tune,
As we burn a treat—did we start a ruin?

In snowball bands, we form our team,
Launching fluff with a gleeful scream.
The neighbors watch with laughter tight,
As we declare a 'snowy' fight!

So come on out, and join the fun,
Under this sky, we all can run.
In frosty air, our spirits lift,
Laughter's the real winter gift.

Snowflakes in Twilight's Embrace

A snowflake lands right on my nose,
I chuckle at its chilly pose.
With friends nearby, we play with glee,
Who knew that snow would set us free?

The hot chocolate stands by with cheer,
But now it's cold; let's all draw near.
With whipped cream hats and smiles so wide,
We sip, we laugh, our hearts collide.

Sleds whisking 'round, oh what a sight,
We race down hills till the stars are bright.
With every bounce, we giggle and shout,
Let's do it again, without a doubt!

So here's to fun in winter's embrace,
Where laughs and mishaps fill every space.
In frosty air, we'll dance, we'll sing,
As snowflakes fall and joy takes wing.

The Quietness of a Sleeping World

Snowflakes flutter, light and spry,
Frogs confused, they croak, oh my!
Bears in dreams, they dance and spin,
While penguins rock, let the fun begin!

Icicles hang like teeth of a grin,
Squirrels in sweaters, they burst out in chin.
The rabbit's hop, an awkward ballet,
While snowmen giggle, they call it a day.

Hot cocoa spills, oh what a mess,
A cat in the snow, done dressed to impress.
The world's so quiet, what a funny sight,
As snowflakes fall through the crisp, chilly night.

Twinkling Silhouettes in the Snow

Every shadow plays a game of hide,
With snowmen posing, and reindeer slide.
A penguin slips, oh what a fall,
While trees wear caps, they're having a ball!

Stars above with a twinkle and tease,
Shooting across, they make one sneeze.
A snowball flies, but oh what a wuss,
It lands on a dog, now that's a fuss!

The moon peeks in, with a sly little grin,
As winter critters start to spin.
Hopscotch in frost, what a sight it be,
In a snowy field, dancing with glee!

Ventures into the Frigid Abyss

Hats all crooked, mittens mismatched,
Adventures wait where laughter is hatched.
The three-legged dog takes a wild sprint,
While penguins chat, they call it a hint!

A yeti's out, with a sneeze so loud,
While snowflakes swirl, they gather a crowd.
Chasing snowflakes, they frolic and roll,
But watching the cat, that's the ultimate goal!

Snowball fights break with giggles and shouts,
The deer leap high, as cheers round about.
The cold's a game, with friends by my side,
Together we laugh, and the chill's our guide!

Beneath the Canopy of Twinkling Lights

Twinkling bulbs in frosty air,
A cat climbs high, without a care.
The dog does dance in a festive way,
As stars above look down and play.

Tinsel hangs where snowflakes meet,
A squirrel darts, with nimble feet.
The cocoa's warm, the cookies bright,
As laughter swells, filling the night.

Glistening laughter fills the space,
As friends catch snowflakes on their face.
The night's alive with every cheer,
In frosty fun, we hold each dear!

Chasing Shadows in the Silver Chill

In a field so cold and bright,
I chased my hat that took to flight.
It danced around like it was free,
I begged it back; it laughed at me.

Snowmen giggle, scarves askew,
Their button eyes say, "Look at you!"
I tried to join their frosty fray,
But fell face-first into the bay.

The moon is grinning wide tonight,
As ice skates slip; what a sight!
The penguins cheer, they give a hoot,
While I'm tangled like a root.

A snowball flies, it finds my nose,
I stumble back, and down I goes!
In winter's charm, we laugh and play,
Just try to avoid a slick ballet.

Tales from the Stellar Frost

Up on the roof, a raccoon prances,
He steals my snacks with cheeky glances.
I tried to shoo him, wave a hand,
He looked at me like I'm quite bland.

The trees wear coats of sparkling white,
As squirrels plot their nutty flight.
They scurry fast, with fluffy tails,
The neighbors think they're tiny whales!

Cold winds hum tunes, a frosty beat,
While I dance around in two left feet.
I spin so hard, I trip and fall,
The ice says, "That's not how we ball!"

Under the stars, mischief glows,
As laughter floats, and chaos flows.
What a night for tales and jest,
In frosty realms, we're truly blessed.

A Waltz Among the Winter Orbs

Out in the yard, a snowball fight,
My friends and I bring all our might.
We hurl and tumble; oh, what a scene,
The dogs just wag, all loud and keen.

A swirling dance with chilly grace,
We trip and slide, a wild chase.
My glove's a sponge, it soaks right through,
While I twirl like a flapped-up stew.

The stars above are in on the fun,
They twinkle bright when the day is done.
I wink at them; they wink right back,
The universe is on this track!

With laughter loud, we spin and glide,
In this frosty ball, we take great pride.
So here we are, in goofy ranks,
Where winter waltzes and chuckles pranks.

The Glittering Veil of Night's Grip

The stars are wearing shiny hats,
While I slip and slide on frozen mats.
My nose is red, just like a flare,
But laughter lifts me in the air.

A snowman strikes a goofy pose,
With carrot nose and painted toes.
He cracks a joke, we all will roar,
Until he topples—splat!—the floor!

At nighttime's glow, we're out to play,
The chilly breath keeps cold at bay.
With mittens on and spirits bright,
We dance and sing into the night.

When frosty winds begin to tease,
We cling to joy like winter's breeze.
This glitter's warmth, we tuck in tight,
And share the fun 'neath the stars' light.

Starlit Resilience in the Cold

In the frost a snowman sings,
As squirrels wear their fuzzy bling.
A penguin slips on ice so slick,
And wobbles like a party trick.

The stars above, they wink and tease,
While snowflakes fall like jokes, with ease.
The chilly night brings giggles near,
As winter skies laugh in good cheer.

Hot cocoa spills with silly grace,
Marshmallows floating in a race.
Snowball fights amid the chill,
Who knew cold could be such a thrill?

So let the winter giggles reign,
With frosty grins, we'll dance through rain.
Stars above will spark our glee,
In this icy jubilee!

Celestial Echoes Above Chilled Slumber

The moon is grinning, what a sight,
A pancake flipped in pure delight.
Shooting stars like sausages fall,
Made me laugh at the dinner call.

Cuddled close, we share a shrug,
While blankets tickle, soft and snug.
Whispers of chilly winds proclaim,
That winter's here to play its game.

Slippers squeak on frosty floors,
As cats play tag with winter's doors.
The laughter echoes through the room,
As stars above begin to bloom.

With starlit chuckles filling the night,
We sip our warmth, all feels just right.
In chilly silence, giggles burst,
An icy world that makes us thirst.

The Frozen Trail of Stars

Footprints crunch on sparkling snow,
As squirrels dance in the moonlit glow.
A comet zips, a funny face,
Blasting through the cosmic race.

Frosty noses, all aglow,
With laughter chasing winter's flow.
Snowflakes pirouette on high,
Like ballerinas in the sky.

Hot soup spills with winter cheer,
While polar bears crack jokes so dear.
Each twinkle sparks a playful grin,
In this frozen game, we all win.

So roast the marshmallows, let them char,
As we gather 'neath the twinkling stars.
With every giggle, the night's our stage,
Cold can't stop this joyful page!

Melancholy of Starlit Frost

The frost is sad, it winks and sighs,
As snowflakes tumble from chilly skies.
I asked a snowman how he's feeling,
He smiled wide, with frozen healing.

Stars twinkle softly, like comic books,
With pinches of humor in their hooks.
A glum penguin slides with style,
As winter's chill stretches a smile.

The Northern Lights play peek-a-boo,
While ice skaters laugh, it's true.
Each crack of ice, a joke unspun,
Who knew the cold could be such fun?

With frosty breaths, we share our fears,
But jokes about ice melt away the tears.
So let's laugh under the shimmering dome,
In this world of cold, we find our home!

The Silent Embrace of Twinkling Light.

In the dark, a snowman sneezes,
His carrot nose, it quakes and teases.
The icicles laugh, oh what a sight,
As they dance with joy, in the pale moonlight.

Penguins in tuxedos, strut with flair,
While snowsuits on kids, are quite the scare.
Sleds zoom by, with giggles at play,
As hot cocoa spills, what a wild display!

The stars twinkle back, with mischief in mind,
Mapping a route for the fun-loving kind.
A snowball whizzed, hits a giant tree,
The tree shakes, grumbling, "Why not aim for me?"

Of frosty delights, the night's full of cheer,
As laughter erupts, our worries disappear.
So grab your mittens, and don your warm hats,
Let's frolic and tumble like playful spats!

Silent Glacier Whispers

The glacier grumbles, a comical joke,
As penguins waddle, like an old oak.
Snowflakes giggle, twirling all about,
While icebergs shimmy, with a frosty shout.

Frosty beasts share secrets, quite bizarre,
A polar bear juggles, under a star.
While seals are singing, in a silly choir,
The chilly jokes take us higher and higher.

An igloo's door creaks, it's quite the scene,
A llama appears, dressed as a queen.
With laughter that echoes, through the frosty air,
Glacier whispers tickle, with a frosty flair.

Oh winter nights, full of fun and light,
With frosty friends, we'll frolic till night.
In a flurry of snow, we tumble and glide,
Together we'll laugh, our worries subside!

Frostbitten Dreams of Night

In frozen lands, where snowmen roam,
A rabbit in boots claims this place his home.
With each little hop, he sends up a spray,
Of giggles all around, chasing worries away.

A snowflake flops, landing near the fire,
And laughs at the warmth that it can't acquire.
While reindeer prance, with shoes not quite right,
Shoelaces untied in the beautiful night.

The skiers descend like stars out of space,
Spinning and twirling with style and grace.
Until one takes flight, in a snow-laden arc,
Landing face-first, igniting a spark!

Yet through all the chaos and icy cold chill,
The laughter erupts and the spirits stay still.
For in dreams of frost, our joy takes flight,
As we dance through the evening and savor the night!

Celestial Frost

The stars twinkle bright, like a sparkling show,
While snowflakes descend, with a pirouette flow.
A cat in a scarf watches the parade,
As chimneys puff smoke, in a comical cascade.

The moon plays peek-a-boo, hiding its glow,
While rabbits in goggles prepare for a bowl.
They bounce on the ice, with absolute glee,
Creating a ruckus beneath the old tree.

Frosty cupcakes await by the fireplace,
While a squirrel in mittens has claimed them with grace.
He spins on his tail, and the party ignites,
With snacks flying wildly through magical nights.

In laughter we bask, as the chill starts to bite,
With friends all around, it feels just right.
Dancing and spinning under celestial frost,
For the joy of the night, oh, we are never lost!

Twinkling Hopes in the Snow

A snowman waves with a carrot nose,
He lost his hat to a gusty pose.
Sleds fly by like giant birds,
While down the hill, we trade our words.

Snowflakes dance like they're on air,
Hot cocoa spills—oh, what a scare!
The chill hangs out, we joke and tease,
Our cheeks are red, we laugh with ease.

Frosty friends, they start to sway,
In the frosty breeze, they play all day.
The sun peeks out just for a glance,
And all the snowflakes join the dance.

With every laugh, the winter's bright,
In cozy rooms, we share delight.
As stars pop out, it's time to cheer,
For all the joy that comes each year.

Galaxy's Whisper on Frosted Ground

A tiny snowflake slips and slides,
It lands right on my cat's great pride.
He leaps and bounds as if on cue,
What's this? A snowball? Oh, boo-hoo!

The night is bright with stars that twinkle,
As we try to avoid that prickly wrinkle.
Faces covered in snow so white,
It's hard to tell who's wrong or right.

We throw snowballs—what a sight!
Missed my target! Oh, such a fright!
But laughter echoes in the night,
This frosty fun is pure delight.

A galaxy above, we look in awe,
Yet here on earth, we cling to our flaw.
In silliness, warmth, we've found our tune,
As friends stem laughter under the moon.

Winter's Hushed Soliloquy

The icicles hang like jester's crowns,
They shimmer with joy, our winter gowns.
A squirrel scurries for a hidden nut,
Under the snow, he takes a cut.

We build a fort, and giggles start,
We launch our attacks with frozen art.
Snowball fights, a grand old fling,
The winter's call feels like a spring.

Hushed moments come, we catch our breath,
As snowflakes whisper tales of wealth.
The world pauses under the night,
And laughter glimmers in the light.

With every breath, a chilly puff,
We giggle still, though it's quite rough.
Let's dance 'til dawn, with all our zest,
In this winter fair, we're truly blessed.

Starshine on Upper Crystal Skies

The stars above wink down so bright,
While I tumble in snow, what a sight!
My mittens lost to a fluffy heap,
In wintry bliss, I lose my sleep.

A penguin strolls—it's quite absurd,
With an ice-cream cone? Have you heard?
We chat about the frosty scenes,
While plotting world domination with beans!

Snowmen gather for a midnight chat,
With funny tales from a floppy hat.
Each flake shines like a tiny joke,
With every giggle, we provoke.

Under the moon's theatrical glow,
Our laughter rings through the falling snow.
We'll twirl and whirl, our spirits high,
In this winter play, we'll never say goodbye.

Under the Celestial Canopy

In the cold, I wore my hat,
A squirrel thought I was a cat.
He scampered up onto my knee,
I laughed so hard, he ran from me.

Snowflakes fell like tiny snowballs,
Tickling noses, oh what fun calls!
A penguin tried to slide on ice,
But landed right in my hot spice!

Stars above began to twinkle,
Frosty cheeks began to crinkle.
A snowman with a carrot nose,
Took a selfie—then struck a pose!

Hot cocoa steam began to rise,
A snowball fight? Oh, what a surprise!
With laughter echoing through the chill,
I dodged and laughed and felt the thrill!

Midnight's Icy Dance

The moon was shining like a lamp,
A polar bear made quite a stamp.
He danced around, all in a spin,
Looked like a furry, clumsy kin.

Snowflakes waltzed in sync, so tight,
While rabbits hopped with pure delight.
A snowshoe hare tried to moonwalk,
But tangled up, forgot his talk!

Icicles hung like frozen chimes,
Making music of wintery rhymes.
Nearby, a chicken tried to skate,
But slipped and slid on fate's first date!

In the dark, the stars all winked,
While frostbite teased, as laughter linked.
We twirled and spun under the night,
A snowy dance floor, what a sight!

Glimmering Dreams of Ice

I woke up in a snowy maze,
Tangled up in my flannel craze.
Outside, a snowman wore my shoe,
His carrot nose asked, 'Hey, who are you?'

Frosty whispers filled the air,
While squirrels plotted without a care.
A penguin pulled out his ice skates,
And teased a panda who couldn't wait!

Stars above began to twinkle bright,
While laughter echoed through the night.
A cat in a scarf made quite the scene,
Chasing shadows, look at her gleam!

With dreaming minds, we built our fort,
No need for summer's warm consort.
In this frosty, glimmering land,
Joyous chaos—come take my hand!

Haiku of the Silent Night

Snowflakes whisper soft,
Turtles take a jog, quite slow,
Winter's breath is loud.

Laughter in the dark,
Snowmen tumble with delight,
Stars giggle above.

Chickens in warm coats,
Dance along the frosty trail,
Pigs dream of hot days.

Frozen dreams unfold,
While hot cocoa warms the soul,
Nature's funny dance.

The Flicker of Distant Lights

In the chilly night, we dance so bright,
Frostbite bites, but we laugh in delight.
The stars twinkle like they've lost their clout,
While snowflakes swirl, giving us a shout!

Mittens mismatched, we look quite the sight,
With noses red, we're a funny plight.
A snowman grins with a carrot nose,
But he melts faster than our playful woes!

Sleds go flying, oh what a thrill,
But someone tumbles, and it's quite the spill.
We giggle hard, it's our winter game,
Chasing each other, it's never the same!

So here we are, with our frosty cheer,
In the moon's glow, without a single fear.
The flicker of lights guides us tonight,
As we frolic and play till the morning light!

Solstice Secrets Unveiled

Gather 'round, come hear the tale,
Of winter nights, when the snowflakes sail.
We whisper secrets, not so profound,
Like why hot cocoa never leaves the ground!

The yuletide log crackles, it's quite the show,
While the cat's on the mantle, all ready to go.
He jumps for the lights, oh what a disaster,
But we laugh it off, it's a holiday master!

With cookies adorned in artistic designs,
We bake and we munch, on sweet, sugary lines.
Turns out the sprinkles taste like regret,
As we wonder why we haven't learned yet!

In this solstice glow, we jest and tease,
Making snow angels, with such silly ease.
Clumsy and carefree, we laugh as we sway,
Unveiling the secrets of this festive play!

Chasing Shadows of the Moon

Tonight we chase shadows, oh what a game,
With our silly antics, we're never the same.
The moon's a spotlight on our frosty caps,
We tumble and roll, in our snowy maps!

The owls up above give a hoot and a wink,
As we build snow forts, don't you dare blink!
Snowballs like missiles, we aim with great glee,
But I'd watch my back if I were you, see!

In a flurry of laughter, we slip and we slide,
As the wintry winds carry us with pride.
Our boots are too big, what a sight to behold,
But nothing can stop us from being bold!

So here's to the night of shadows and fun,
With cheeks rosy red, we'll run till we're done.
Chasing shadows, under the moon's bright gaze,
In this jolly frolic, we'll always amaze!

A Blanket of Crystal Silence

Wrapped up snug, in a blanket of white,
The world is quiet, yet we're ready to bite.
But wait! What's that? A sound from the bush,
Could it be squirrels having a rush?

With helmets made out of snow and pure fun,
We valiantly march, no sign of a run.
But icy surprise waits just at my feet,
And down I go, with a comical beat!

As the stars peep down through branches like spies,
We create snow angels, oh how we rise!
But landing soft doesn't go as we plan,
As snow cascades down with a laugh from the man.

So let's embrace this crystal still night,
With chuckles and giggles, until morning light.
In our winter wonderland, let's make some noise,
For laughter is best, in this land of joys!

The Cold Lullaby of the Heavens

The sky hums a frosty tune,
Where snowflakes dance like a cartoon.
With icicles hanging like teeth in a grin,
The cold laughs at warmth, oh where have you been?

A snowman wobbles, cheeks of coal,
Claiming he's on a frosty stroll.
But with each step, he starts to melt,
And wonders why he's never felt a belt!

In mittens too big, kids flail and slip,
A toboggan ride ends with a flip.
They giggle and squeal, what a silly sight,
As they tumble back down into snow so white!

Stars twinkle with laughter, high up above,
Perhaps they're singing, or just spreading love.
So let's snuggle tight, wrapped in blankets too,
And dream of warm beaches, with skies ever blue.

Northern Lights and Frosted Paths

The sky's a canvas, colors on spill,
Like a painter lost in a winter thrill.
Green, pink, and purple, a dizzying show,
It's like Mother Nature had too much snow!

Footprints lead to nowhere, zigzagging around,
While squirrels throw snowballs, they're silly and bound.
One lands on a cat, all fluffy and mad,
It's a purr-fect disaster, oh what fun to be had!

Frosty breath dances like playful ghosts,
As penguin-tipped mittens raise chilly toasts.
To hot cocoa and marshmallows, round and sweet,
While snowflakes sneak in, heading straight for our feet!

With laughter echoing through crisp, starry nights,
On paths full of mischief and cheesy delights.
We'll dodge the frostbite, just keep up the cheer,
As long as there's laughter, there's nothing to fear!

Whispers of Icy Journeys

A sled rides down, then takes to the air,
With a twist and a turn, oh, beware, beware!
Through snow-dusted bushes and over a hill,
The laughter that follows gives everyone a thrill.

Frosty whispers ooze from every branch,
As snowflakes swirl in a winter dance.
They chat about snowmen, how one lost a hat,
That tumbled and bounced — what a humorous spat!

The moon peeks down, with a wink and a nod,
At frozen marshmallows, extra chewy and odd.
Hot chocolate dreams in tall mugs of cheer,
With a sprinkle of giggles that warms the cold sheer.

So come, let's jest with the snowflakes aglow,
And map out the places only we seem to know.
With rosy cheeks shining, we'll dance in delight,
As the stars chuckle softly, all through the night!

Secrets Written in Snow

Forget the ink, it's the snow that writes,
With secrets of laughter and playful delights.
A snowball note may just land on your face,
And the giggles that follow, well, that's a warm trace!

Snowflakes fall like whispers from above,
Each one unique, but oh, how they shove!
Down children's jackets and into their mittens,
Who knew winter could be so full of kittens?

Winter's a prankster in many a way,
Making kids tumble and frolic in play.
With a curious dog and a tree full of pine,
There's mischief afoot, oh is it not fine?

As night softly wraps up like a cozy old quilt,
Stars share the gossip of snowmen they built.
With snickers from orbs that hang in the black,
Winter's dance is a joy that we just can't lack!

Snowflakes Kiss the Sky

Tiny flakes that dance and swirl,
I tripped and made a snowy whirl!
They giggle as they touch my nose,
A cold surprise, the fun just grows.

Snowmen stand with goofy grins,
They wear my scarf, and that's a win!
As snowballs fly like wild confetti,
My aim is off — oh, isn't that petty?

The world is white, a frosty joke,
My sledding skills, oh, what a poke!
I zig and zag, but mostly fall,
Laughing at the winter's call.

With mittens on that barely fit,
I throw a snowball — what a hit!
The stars above shine bright and clear,
While I'm the one who has no cheer!

Dreams Trapped in Crystal Light

In a world of frosty delight,
My dreams were caught in shimmering light.
But chasing them is quite the spree,
They run away, oh, woe is me!

I thought I'd catch a star or two,
Instead, I tripped on a rubber shoe!
The snowflakes giggle, oh what a tease,
They swirl around me in winter's breeze.

Awake or caught in a frosty dream,
I launched a snowball; it missed — what a scream!
They laugh and dance in a chilly parade,
While I'm left standing, utterly dismayed.

With my nose bright red, it's clear to see,
That winter's magic is mocking me.
Yet I can't help but laugh at the plight,
Dreams trapped in laughter, shining bright!

A Stillness etched in Starlight

In quiet nights, when snowflakes land,
The world turns soft, like a fluffy band.
Yet in that stillness, a sneeze breaks through,
A snowman shudders — who's that, boo-hoo?

The stars above, they twinkle bold,
While I'm stuck with mittens, way too cold.
I think I saw one wink at me,
Is that a joke or just my glee?

Snowballs are aimed at unwitting friends,
Their laughter echoes; the fun never ends!
But footsteps crunch, it's hard to sneak,
Who knew winter chill could feel so cheek?

I dream of spring, though winter's dear,
With sparkling nights to keep us near.
Through laughter and snow, my heart feels light,
Etched with joy in that starlit night!

The Celestial Whisper of Night's Breath

The sky's a canvas, dark and deep,
With stars that wink and softly creep.
Yet winter's breath is quite the tease,
It makes me laugh, it makes me sneeze!

I tried to catch a falling star,
But hit my head, oh, that was bizarre!
The cosmos giggles, its glitter shines,
As snowflakes play hopscotch on the pines.

I built a fort that's broad and stout,
But snow fell in — oh, what a clout!
With each fresh flake, my fort's a blur,
I pull it down, and giggles stir.

The moon yells down, "Hey, what's the fuss?"
I say, "Just fun, you can join us!"
So together we laugh under celestial glee,
As winter nights bring joy to me!

Shadows Frozen in Time

In a land where snowflakes spin,
Socks are missing, none can win.
A snowman wearing grandpa's hat,
Sips on cocoa, how about that?

Fido slides on his furry bum,
Chasing flakes, oh what fun!
He jumps and slips, what a sight,
Howling at the moon so bright!

Icicles hang like musical chimes,
I hum a tune to frosty rhymes.
The trees wear blankets, all cozy and bright,
While squirrels plot a snowball fight!

Time stands still, or so they say,
When winter comes to play all day.
But watch your step, it's a slippery spree,
You might just laugh at your own two knees!

The Breath of Cosmic Winter

A snowflake winks from the sky,
Did it just giggle, oh my?
The stars above gossip with glee,
As I slip on ice, whee! Whee!

Chasing comets on a sled,
Imagining all the things I've said.
"Watch out!" I shout, but the dog just flies,
With a sparkly coat, oh how he tries!

The moon guffaws at my frozen dance,
Only to take its own chance.
A slip, a slide, a tumble so wide,
Who needs dignity, joy is the guide!

Hidden in snowballs, giggles confine,
A cosmic twist, everyone's divine.
So grab a glove, let's make some cheer,
In a winter wonderland filled with jests and sneers!

Illuminated Frost

The frost bites sharp, yet here I stand,
With a glow-stick and a snowball in hand.
I dance around in a twinkling spree,
Who knew icicles could cause such glee?

A penguin waddles with style so grand,
"Do the worm!" it tells me, isn't that planned?
We groove on ice, a slippery feat,
I spin and twirl, what a chilly treat!

Glistening trees look like they're pranked,
With ornaments gone from last year's bank.
But they squeak with laughter, they know it's true,
Winter's joke is always on you!

So let's paint the night in frosty hues,
With shimmery snow and whimsical views.
Joy is scattered like sprinkles of frost,
Let's embrace the silly, never the lost!

The Winter's Ethereal Veil

A veil of snowflakes covers the ground,
I wonder if penguins can dance around?
Elves in sleds are zooming past,
"Watch out, Frosty!" they squeal at last!

Winding pathways made of ice,
I did a pirouette, oh so nice!
But fell on my butt with a hilarious thud,
Now I'm stuck in the cold, a snow angel crud.

The hare hops by with a carrot gun,
"Let's start a revolution, this will be fun!"
But I just laugh, as he darts away,
Wishing for cocoa, at the end of the day.

So grab that mitt, come join my quest,
To sled through the hills, it's the very best!
Under the luminous moon's gentle embrace,
We'll giggle together, in this wintry race!

Sleet's Serenade

Little ice crystals dance in the night,
Misshapen snowmen such a funny sight.
They wobble and wobble, no chance to stand,
A frosty parade in this winter land.

Snowflakes fall down, a soft tickle fight,
Icicles hanging, sharp and polite.
They glimmer and shine like giants' teeth,
But one little slip, and down goes my wreath!

Mittens and scarves, all tangled in glee,
The dog thinks it's time for an epic spree.
He's rolled in the snow, then ran like a flash,
Now he's a snowball, gone with a splash!

A sledding adventure, the hills call my name,
But what's that? My pants have joined in the game!
Who knew frosty fun could end in such flair?
With laughter and tumbles, we float like the air.

Celestial Guardians of Winter

Stars like snowflakes sprinkle the sky,
While socks go missing, oh my, oh my!
Laundry's a puzzle, so odd and so round,
Yet still we all giggle, confusion abound.

Snowmen wear hats and scarves that are bright,
With carrots for noses, but oh what a sight!
One leans too far and falls with a thud,
"Catch me if you can!" he yells with a bud.

Penguins in coats slip and slide all around,
They gather a crowd, what a wintery sound!
"Do the cha-cha!" one shouts; the audience roars,
As they waddle and jiggle, dodging snow floors.

Galactic giggles echo very well,
As we sip hot cocoa and rings of marshmallow.
Under this laugh-filled, twinkling abyss,
We revel in chaos, pure wintery bliss.

The Quietude of Starlit Snow

The moon giggles softly through branches of frost,
While squirrels argue about the nuts that they lost.
In snow-laden trees, rabbits bink in delight,
Chasing each other 'til they vanish from sight.

Mistakes made by snowflakes, they flutter and fall,
"Oops, wrong roof," says one, "I'm off to the mall!"
Snowdrifts are sneaky, they hide with a grin,
I nearly trip over; oh, where to begin?

A feathered brigade, the birds in a line,
Debate in a flurry on who's next to dine.
As the snow gently blankets the world oh so bright,
Even winter's chaos is wrapped up so tight.

With giggles and whispers that lighten the air,
We crunch and we stumble, with laughter to spare.
The warmth in our hearts makes this moment so right,
Together we bask in the softening night.

Bathing in Frost Light

Twinkling frost on my windows does play,
Like glittering friends who have come out to stay.
The cat's on the sill, giving stink eye to snow,
"Why do they steal all the light? Don't they know?"

A snowball revolt, they gather in force,
"To battle the kids! It's a winterly course!"
But the kids are too quick; they duck and they dive,
While the snowmen cheer, alive and contrived.

Pine trees wear sweaters, knit tight and pulled high,
While laughter erupts like a kite in the sky.
The frolicsome chill wraps us light as a dream,
As we dance in the shadows, together we beam.

What's that? A snow angel, a flap and a plop!
"Make room for the seal!" with a giggle and hop.
Frozen splendor, with sparkle and cheer,
In this frosty bath, we've no room for fear.

Echoing Footprints on Frozen Paths

Little feet crunch on the snow,
Chasing a dog that won't say no.
Laughter rings through the frosty air,
As mittens vanish without a care.

Snowballs fly like crazy darts,
Dodging snowmen with silly parts.
One wrong throw, and down I fall,
Covered in frost, I can't stand tall.

Sleds zoom past with cheerful squeals,
Launching kids with icy wheels.
A hot cocoa must, oh what a treat,
While toes sit warming by the heat.

Wiggle your toes, give your nose a rub,
Let's feast on marshmallows in the tub.
With giggles echoing, we'll reminisce,
About slippery moments and winter bliss.

Constellations in the Snow

Starlight twinkles on fluffy ground,
As we make angels without a sound.
Who knew snowflakes had such flair,
When they land on our noses and hair?

Mapping the skies with hot cocoa and sips,
Chasing shooting stars with icy fingertips.
We'll build a rocket from snow and cheer,
Ready for launch in the frosty sphere.

Snowman has glasses, a carrot nose,
In his top hat, a story grows.
With eyes made of coal and a grin so wide,
He's the funniest dude in this chilly ride.

So let's dance among the frozen glow,
As constellations whisper secrets below.
While the world slumbers under a thick quilt,
We'll laugh 'til we snort with joy we've built.

Cosmic Chill

I step outside in my fluffy gear,
Wondering why winter brings me cheer.
The frosty air tickles my toes,
And tangled up, my scarf just grows.

Snowflakes fall like tiny stars,
Hitting my head like little cars.
I spin around, arms open wide,
Like an astronaut lost in snow, I glide.

A friendly snowball hits my cheek,
That mischievous grin makes me weak.
But before I could launch one back,
I slip and fall, oh what a knack!

Polar bears waddle in my mind,
As I trip on ice, foot unaligned.
But laughter echoes in this chill,
Winter's a playground, and we've got skill.

Earthly Warmth

Footprints tracing laughter's dance,
In this cold, we take a chance.
A snowman's hat looks a bit askew,
With carrots poking out, kind of a view!

The hot cocoa bubbled, like sweet delight,
Marshmallows turn ninja with each bite.
Let's toast to mittens lost in drifts,
Through comic mishaps, our spirits lift.

A dance-off begins on the ice so thick,
We swirl and twirl, think we're slick.
But one little slip, and down I land,
With laughter ringing, my pride won't stand.

So gather 'round with mugs in hand,
Tell me your quirkiest winterland.
In this frosty party, we all belong,
Wrapped in warmth where we sing our song.

Icy Reflections of a Dream

Mirror-like puddles reflect the night,
Faces all giggling, what a sight!
With frozen toes and joyful hearts,
The icy air gives funny sparks.

A penguin waddle by the tree,
Chasing my friend who laughs with glee.
But oh! She slipped, slid like a pro,
Fell on her back, yelling, "Let it snow!"

Moonlight dances on snowy mounds,
As we compete for silliest sounds.
With snowflakes in hair and big toothy grins,
Let's see who can win this frosty spin!

The night wraps us in laughter and light,
As we share stories, hearts feeling bright.
In the chill, we find warmth, it seems,
In icy reflections of our wild dreams.

Journey Through the Crystal Quiet

In a world made of snow and ice,
The squirrels wear hats, oh so nice.
Penguins slide, a perfect show,
While snowmen dance, moving slow.

Laughter echoes, the moon does grin,
As snowflakes fall and the fun begins.
A rabbit slips, oh what a sight,
Then bounces back with all its might.

Hot chocolate brews, the marshmallows float,
While frosty critters start to gloat.
With snowball fights and giggles galore,
Who knew winter could spark such uproar?

So grab your skates, let's take a twirl,
And watch as chilly snowflakes swirl.
Love this season? You bet your boots!
It's funny how frost can bring such hoots!

Canvas of Stars and Snowflakes

A canvas white, with dots of light,
The stars are winking, what a sight!
A polar bear with a hat so big,
Struts his stuff, busting a jig.

Snowflakes tumble, each one a dance,
While hedgehogs prance in winter's trance.
A cat in mittens, what a fancy feat,
Chases its tail, then takes a seat.

The owls are plotting a snowball game,
While winter winds whisper their names.
With starlit giggles, they join the fray,
Creating frosty fun in their own way.

So join the fun, don't miss the play,
Let laughter rule this snowy day.
With stars that sparkle and snowflakes twirl,
Who knew winter could be such a whirl?

Cosmic Chill in the Night

Cosmic chill, a frosty breeze,
The rabbits wear sweaters, oh please!
Dancing shadows under the moonlight glow,
Even the snowmen flex with a 'whoa!'

A penguin takes a slide on ice,
Yelling "Wheeee!" isn't that nice?
While comets zoom with a trail so bright,
Ice slides shine, it's such a delight.

The owls are hooting a silly tune,
Dressed in shades looking quite immune.
With hot cocoa spilled and giggles shared,
These frosty friends declare they've fared.

So chill with me in this cosmic space,
Where laughter blooms, and we embrace.
With frostbit toes and smiles so wide,
Who would have thought winter's got such pride?

The Nightingale of Frost

The nightingale sings with a frosty beak,
While chipmunks dance, so sleek and chic.
Twinkling stars laugh at their moves,
As snowflakes swirl, the night improves.

The critters gather, a silly choir,
Giggling loudly, never tire.
A moose in pajamas joins the fun,
Under the glow of the chilly sun.

With cocoa cups and snow so bright,
Squirrels are surfing on ice tonight.
Winter's a party, don't you see?
We're all just players in this spree.

So join the nightingale, take your chance,
In this frosty world, let's all prance.
With laughter echoed through crisp air,
Who knew winter could be this rare?

Harmony of Cold and Light

In the snowflakes, we find a dance,
Hats on heads, we prance and prance.
A snowball fight turns into a freeze,
Laughter echoes among the trees.

Frosted branches hold silly sights,
Penguins waddle in fuzzy tights.
A snowman grins with a carrot nose,
Wishing he had a pair of toes!

Sleds zoom by with a woosh and a laugh,
A crash that leads to the best photograph.
Hot chocolate cheers on a chilly spree,
Life's a hoot, come join the glee!

The moon peeks out with a twinkling grin,
As frozen antics make all hearts spin.
With frosty fingers, we wave goodbye,
To winter skies that make us sigh.

Twilight's Whisper Under Ice

The sun dips low in a frosty coat,
Bunny hops in a scarf—what a sight!
Icicles dangle, sharp as a joke,
As we slide on the ice, oh what a fright!

Whispers of ice, they giggle and cheer,
While penguins gossip about snowflakes near.
A squirrel twirls, too proud to fall,
Braving the cold, he's the king of them all.

We build a fort and host a grand feast,
Snowflakes dance like they're at the least.
Muffin crumbs lead to a cheeky surprise,
Squirrels stealing treats right before our eyes!

With stars that chuckle in the night,
And snowmen trying to hold their fright,
We laugh till we stumble, hearts all aglow,
Under the twilight, we steal the show.

The Veil of Frozen Dreams

A blanket of white covers the town,
Invisible creatures all around.
Underfoot crunch, the sound is divine,
As snowflakes tickle and start to align.

A cat in boots with a snowy cap,
Dreaming of fish in a frosty nap.
While raccoons wear scarves that are far too tight,
Trying to fashion their own winter flight.

Hot cider giggles as it steams in the mug,
While mittens play tag with a warm winter hug.
Carrot noses get lost in the fray,
Snow shovels dance and decide to play.

As stars giggle in the velvet sky,
Icy dreams swirl, no reason to sigh.
With laughter, mischief, a chilly embrace,
In the night's sweet embrace, we find our place.

Stars Above, Silence Below

Stars twinkle down on a snowy white stage,
A snowflake flops on a bunny's leg.
Frosty whiskers, oh what a tease,
A shout and a tumble, I'm lost in the freeze!

Snowmen gossip, their noses askew,
While deer laugh softly, they know what to do.
In the snowfall's hush, fun hides and creeps,
Did you hear the one about the snowball that sleeps?

With snowflakes twirling in dizzy delight,
And penguins searching for socks in the night.
Hot soup is served with giggles and cheer,
At this winter's party, happiness is here!

With stars that twinkle and winks even bigger,
We hop and we skip, our eyes all aglitter.
In the frosty whispers, our spirits soar high,
In a world made of laughter under a cold sky.